PAMPHLETS ON AMERICAN WRITERS · NUMBER 16

UNIVERSITY OF MINNESOTA

Recent American Poetry

BY GLAUCO CAMBON

UNIVERSITY OF MINNESOTA PRESS · MINNEAPOLIS

Printed in the United States of America at the
Lund Press, Inc., Minneapolis

Library of Congress Catalog Card Number: 62-62784

second printing 1965

PUBLISHED IN GREAT BRITAIN, INDIA, AND PAKISTAN BY THE OXFORD
UNIVERSITY PRESS, LONDON, BOMBAY, AND KARACHI, AND IN
CANADA BY THOMAS ALLEN, LTD., TORONTO

RECENT AMERICAN POETRY

GLAUCO CAMBON is a professor of comparative literature at Rutgers University and a fellow of the Indiana School of Letters. A native of Italy, he is the author of verse, essays, and criticism in both Italian and English.

⤻ *Recent*
American Poetry

W RITING in 1950, John Ciardi could say in the foreword to
his anthology of fifteen "mid-century" American poets that bar-
baric yawps à la Whitman, as well as daredevil experimentation,
were through; since the war, especially, the "redskin" poet (to say
it with Philip Rahv) had definitely had to make room for the "pale-
face" and this shift in literary taste found broad confirmation in the
social fact that now American poets flocked to the sheltering uni-
versities. They were finally respectable! Hence the academic tone
of much verse published since the war. Sophistication, irony, prig-
gish detachment were *de rigueur* for every young writer; everybody
knew his Eliot, for yesterday's revolution had become today's insti-
tution. Poetry tended increasingly to be "the subject of the poem"—
with the attendant risk of endogamic sterility.

Chaotically adolescent as it was in many cases, the "Howl" of the
Beat Generation against institutionalized poetry served to adminis-
ter a shock to academic quiescence in the mid-fifties. Poetry does
not necessarily fall into cataleptic slumber in a college classroom,
particularly if the teacher happens to be a Robert Lowell, nor does
a bohemian uniform and beard guarantee its rise from narcosis. But,
in separating itself from the wild twenties and the committed thir-
ties, the mid-century generation risked forgetting that civilization,
especially in literature, is not a matter of suburban comfort. Ener-
getic reminders of this fact in the postwar years came not only from
the Beats: controversial Ezra Pound made no concessions to what
Lowell calls "the tranquillized fifties," as *Rock Drill* and *Thrones*

5

can show, while William Carlos Williams completed his drastically unconventional *Paterson*, thereby supplying (along with Pound) much fire to the youngest generation of literary pioneers — Robert Duncan, Robert Creeley, Denise Levertov, Gary Snyder, not to mention their older partner Kenneth Rexroth; E. E. Cummings refused to "go respectable," and from across the ocean Dylan Thomas brought his own infectious, self-consuming fire.

The mavericks have had their effect, and at this writing the pendulum seems to be swinging again, as evidenced by the fact that poets formerly committed to closed traditional meters and rhythms, like Donald Hall, James Wright, and Lowell himself, are venturing out into open forms, chiefly at the instigation of tameless old Williams. Now, especially, one should beware of simplifying young American verse into Van Wyck Brooks's well-known dichotomy of "highbrow" versus "lowbrow." Take, for example, two rival anthologies like *The New Poets of England and America* and *The New American Poetry, 1945–1960*. A polarity is there, but one does no justice to either group by identifying the former with genteel correctness and the latter with unrestrained wildness: Donald Allen's heterogeneous book includes viable writers who experiment for the sake of a genuine poetical quest rather than to flaunt a by now fashionable Beat pose, while the poets sponsored by Hall, Pack and Simpson are far from complacently tame — indeed they have among them a May Swenson, a Robert Bly, and other "young Turks." And after all, Denise Levertov, Robert Duncan, and Robert Creeley (to name some serious poets anthologized by Allen) have appeared in *Poetry*, a magazine the diehard Beats certainly consider "square." On the American literary scene, palefaces and redskins are fighting it out once again, but each group has, to adopt a sociological metaphor, its "marginal men," crossing the lines.

In this kind of a fluid situation it would be impossible within restricted compass to provide a reliable picture of all strains of post war poetry in the United States. Rather than try to be superficially comprehensive here, it seems advisable to essay some focal sampling of what has been achieved. For beyond the conflicting or overlapping trends, individual achievement is what matters, whatever the proclaimed aesthetics behind it.

Our chosen chronological context excludes the outstanding work of Robert Lowell, whose reputation was already getting established before the postwar period, and the same is true of Karl Shapiro. The former with his prophetic fire, the latter with his variously hearty or embittered response to American reality, are permanent presences not to be ignored, but they cannot be discussed in detail here. Theodore Roethke, whose "words" are really not "for the wind," has likewise not begun his career recently enough, from our point of view, to justify more than a cursory mention, even though it was not until 1958, with the publication of his collected poems, that a broad view of his often exciting, if uneven, endeavor was possible. The "metaphysical" sensibility predominant in modern American verse modulates with him from a Yeatsian strictness of formal statement all the way to a visionary rapture in the Blake manner, which breaks up rhythm and stanza patterns into seemingly loose utterances having only "the shape of fire." The nursery rhymes Roethke includes in his canon are delightfully close to this earnest magic, as they were for Blake, and they subtly confirm his lyrical gift.

Stanley Kunitz, long known as a critic, seems even more eccentric to the scope of our treatment when one reflects that his first book of verse dates from 1930 and his second from 1944. But it was only with the appearance of his *Selected Poems* in 1958 that he achieved the renown he deserves as a poet, and that makes him something like a postwar discovery — belated discoveries being characteristic of American letters. Since he plays for high stakes, it is understandable that he should at times fall into bad taste: overworked metaphors, showy language, shrill tone, and even an occasional touch of drab

7

sentimentality. These are risks he shares with one of his obvious models, Hart Crane, who was never willing to settle for anything less than the lightning of ecstasy. And like Hart Crane, he has learned much from a contemporary, Allen Tate, as well as from that "posthumous" contemporary, Emily Dickinson. See "End of Summer" for evidence of the latter's influence, or "Lovers Relentlessly," or "Geometry of Moods," which recalls Andrew Marvell no less than Emily. At his frequent best, Kunitz attains an electrical crispness of language which finds a natural metric mold in his favorite stanza pattern, the rhymed quatrain Emily Dickinson also loved; there result classical gems like "Deciduous Branch," in which one does not know whether to admire more the crystal hardness of form or its inner vibrancy, while the mystery of the visiting Christ obtains a matchless verbal incarnation in "He." "I Dreamed That I Was Old" is another perfect accomplishment in the closed patterns of classical tradition, but one would not want to pass up the freer final gesture of "The Thief," which strongly concludes a loose narrative of the standard misfortune that befalls many an unwary tourist on a Roman holiday. How refreshing to see a sophisticated craftsman admit he writes for "money, rage, and love"! The mystic (see "Invocation" among other pieces), the literary craftsman, the *engagé* writer ready to protest against injustice, horror, or dullness, and the witty man of the world incredibly coexist in Stanley Kunitz, and realization of this alone may suffice, short of a more thorough analysis, to bring home the momentousness of his contribution to American poetry.

With Richard Wilbur, born in 1921, we come to a fine poet whose publications and success have been entirely a matter of these postwar years. His first three books of verse (*The Beautiful Changes*, 1947; *Ceremony and Other Poems*, 1950; *Things of This World*, 1956) showed no marked change in style, their very constancy of achievement being one of the impressive things about them. (His fourth, *Advice to a Prophet and Other Poems*, 1961, points to some new developments in style.) To the exercise of his art he brought from the start a careful literary training, which has served him well. He certainly knows his classics, Latin, English, or French, but his culture never becomes a dead weight; it rather nourishes his perception in the act of sustaining his awareness of form. Form is first of all the inner "shaping spirit of imagination," without which no poetry happens; but it is best elicited, according to Wilbur, by the provocative resistance of a given pattern, a rigorous meter apt to compel the writer to the suitable verbal choices — and in this he seems to echo the exacting faith of Paul Valéry.

The force of the genie, as Wilbur has it, comes of its being pent up in a bottle, yet this vivid epigram should not mislead anybody into believing that this poet's strength lies in some uneasy tension between "content" and external "form," for his diction shows a rare suppleness. In addition to paying careful attention to the French Symbolists (for whom modern American poets feel a strong affinity, as critic Harold Rosenberg rightly notes) and their resourceful connoisseur Wallace Stevens, Wilbur has closely studied the sinuous rhythms of Marianne Moore: witness the exhilarating expansion of breath he can achieve, within a fixed stanza of his own invention, in an early poem like "Objects":

> Meridians are a net
> Which catches nothing; that sea-scampering bird
> The gull, though shores lapse every side from sight, can yet
> Sense him to land, but Hanno had not heard
>
> Hesperidean song,
> Had he not gone by watchful periploi:
> Chalk rocks, and isles like beasts, and mountain stains along
> The water-hem, calmed him at last near-by

9

> The clear high hidden chant
> Blown from the spellbound coast, where under drifts
> Of sunlight, under plated leaves, they guard the plant
> By praising it. . . .

Here each stanza progressively expands from a short six-syllable first line through the ten syllables of a fairly stable iambic pentameter to attain its diastole in the third line, which may consist of anything from twelve to fifteen syllables; from this climactic expansion the systole begins with a return to the iambic pentameter in the fourth line, until maximum contraction is reached in the first line of the following stanza. This interlocking alternation of movement has nothing mechanical about it, sustained as it is by the run-on lines which create a flow of meaning and music from stanza to stanza, thereby quickening the firm pattern of meter into a series of undulant heaves.

Rhythmical ease perfectly corresponds to the agility of Pindaric transitions from object to object, from perception to perception, from myth to myth, until the felicitous figure of the Phoenician explorer Hanno, that half-mythical forerunner of Vasco da Gama, returns in the end transformed into the discovering consciousness of the poet:

> . . . A quick
> Change of the eye and all this calmly passes
>
> Into a day, into magic.
> . . . .
> . . . Oh maculate, cracked, askew,
>
> Gay-pocked and potsherd world
> I voyage, where in every tangible tree
> I see afloat among the leaves, all calm and curled,
> The Cheshire smile which sets me fearfully free.

Thanks to that unforeseen but wholly appropriate apparition of the Cheshire cat, the poet can define his attitude toward the world as that of Alice toward her Wonderland: wonder and awe. The delightful surprises one keeps meeting in the poem are matched by the basic surprise the poem itself constitutes after the deceptively dry title. An even closer probing into the intimate alliance of rhythm and imagery would bear out how the longest line in the first stanza expresses by its very length the broad sweep of the gull's flight, while its counterpart in the second stanza gives us, through the same device, the encompassing range of the seafarer's eye in its progressive discovery of further horizons.

A similar effect of expansion and recoil animates the elastic stanzas of "Water Walker" (also from *The Beautiful Changes*), a poem which develops into excitingly improbable analogies the theme of the caddis flies "walking on spring-surface, water walkers who breathe / Air and know water." These adaptable insects evoke St. Paul moving between the Hebrew and Graeco-Roman worlds, and the poet himself moving in spirit and body between the mutually incompatible areas of his own native country, North and South, until he becomes "Stranger to both" and discovers "Heaven and hell in the poise / Betwixt 'inhabit' and 'know.'" The writer, like Tonio Kröger in Thomas Mann's novel, is doomed to the difficult privilege of existing "between two worlds," and on that double familiarity which is really a double alienation he must thrive at his own expense, forever seeking to unite or relate, at least in his art, the irreconcilables of life.

An aura of miracle, subtly recalling Christ on the Sea of Galilee, suffuses the entomological cue from the very start when Wilbur, with pregnant exactitude, defines his inspiring bugs as "water walkers." This is only one of the structural felicities in the striking emblem-poem, which boldly sallies forth and returns upon itself at the end, strengthened by a tactful rhyme pattern ("But the dilemma, cherished, tyrannical, / While he despairs and burns / Da capo da capo returns"). There is too the strength of the American language

11

in the poem, and the encompassing way in which the speaking "I" takes in contemporary American reality, sacred and past history, and historyless nature. The twentieth-century sophisticate has Whitman blood in his veins, after all.

American speech contributes its energy to the success of a shorter poem, "Tywater," widely and deservedly anthologized. Cowboy folklore is here used with an unfailing flair, and the four quatrains (partly built on nimble off-rhymes like *ear-air, skill-fell*) have a classical finality of utterance which finds its clincher in the concluding couplet:

> And what to say of him, God knows.
> Such violence. And such repose.

One cannot forget, in this poem, the "lariat's butterfly" of stanza 3, behind which "Shuttled his white and gritted grin, / And cuts of sky would roll within / The noose-hole, when he spun it high." Metaphysical wit here blends to perfection with the American frontier tradition of tall tale and gargantuan humor. At the same time, the finely wrought first stanza, with lines like "Lacking the lily of our Lord, / Alases of the hyacinth," brings to mind Ezra Pound's chiseled "Medallion." That a fusion should actually take place between the two mutually alien styles in this poem is perhaps its greatest title to lasting appreciation. Irony is what makes that fusion possible.

His academic commitments have not insulated Wilbur from such an awareness of the American or broadly modern reality around him as informs pieces like "Mined Country," "First Snow in Alsace," "On the Eyes of an SS Officer," "To an American Poet Just Dead," "He Was," and "For the New Railway Station in Rome." Readers who believe in Matthew Arnold's formula of poetry as criticism of life can see these poems as a defense against the accusation of sterile aestheticism that some critics might conceivably level at the author of couplets like this:

> We milk the cow of the world, and as we do
> We whisper in her ear: "You are not true."

This interest in "epistemology" places Wilbur very close to his American master Wallace Stevens, whose very mannerisms seem to echo here and there in the Alexandrian elegance of his disciple, especially in the poem "Ceremony," the title piece of his second volume:

> A striped blouse in a clearing by Bazille
> Is, you may say, a patroness of boughs . . .

Sometimes it is the title of a poem that calls Stevens to mind: "A Simile for Her Smile," "Five Women Bathing in Moonlight," "La Rose des Vents," " 'A World without Objects Is a Sensible Emptiness,' " "My Father Paints the Summer," "Sunlight Is Imagination," "Praise in Summer," "Attention Makes Infinity." Then we have the entirely Stevensian hankering for the interjection of a French word in the English context: "danseuse," "cigales," "royaume," "bavardage," "travailleur" are ready examples. But Wilbur never falls into whimsicality, as Stevens, for all his genius, often does.

"The Beautiful Changes" recalls Stevens' "Anecdote of a Jar" (and "Notes toward a Supreme Fiction"):

> The beautiful changes as a forest is changed
> By a chameleon's tuning his skin to it;
> As a mantis, arranged
> On a green leaf, grows
> Into it, makes the leaf leafier, and proves
> Any greenness is deeper than anybody knows.

Likewise, "Praise in Summer" vies with Stevens' "The Motive for Metaphor" by questioning the very language of poetry as a (metaphoric) distortion of reality:

> Does sense so stale that it must needs derange
> The world to know it? To a praiseful eye
> Should it not be enough of fresh and strange

> That trees grow green, and moles can course in clay,
> And sparrows sweep the ceiling of our day?

The last line surreptitiously restores the language of metaphor by its clever use of "ceiling," and gives a new turn to the whole poem, lest we be taken in by the claim of matter-of-factness. (Stevens would say that "things as they are / Are changed upon the blue guitar.")

Also strongly reminiscent of Stevens are rich alliterative effects like ". . . the slightest shade of you / Valleys my mind in fabulous blue Lucernes" (from "The Beautiful Changes"), and Stevens' "Bantams in Pine Woods" finds gestural and phonetical echoes in Wilbur's "A Simplification." But at this point, in fairness to Wilbur, one should remember that effects of this kind were frequent in an earlier kindred poet, Emily Dickinson, and, more generally, that Wilbur's concern with mind and the act of knowledge does not derive secondhand from Stevens or Valéry and Mallarmé, since it is ingrained in the Transcendentalist and Puritan tradition of New England, which the New York born poet had no trouble repossessing. It is this that makes Wilbur so susceptible to the French sources Stevens cherished before him, even more than the stylistic exquisiteness which has moved the younger craftsman to emulate as a translator the text of several French lyrics.

An intellectual poet who delights in the visible, Wilbur is as subtly aware of history as Henry James was; a look at "Years-End" will easily prove it. This poem blends a weird awareness of geological time in the immemorial processes of Nature with an apocalyptical sense of the sudden doom that may well impend on us, as it did on so many of our human and animal predecessors, at the end of another seasonal cycle. A "years-end" can imply the end of a whole historical period. Pompeii's mummified inhabitants, the frozen antediluvian mammoths suggestively called "palaces of patience," the obliquely caught implications of our sinister age — everything concurs to set up a mood of clairvoyance. It is as if an immeasurable time were condensed into a single act of consciousness.

Whatever the focus of inspiration — nature, history, or the self-questioning mind — Wilbur can objectify his wonder through a careful craftsmanship which seldom intrudes on the sheer delight of the poem. That is why he can learn from different models (Frost is one, as a reading of "Winter Spring" will show) without succumbing to them. For a poet so conscious of his art, Wilbur is comparatively immune to "artiness." A poem like "The Death of a Toad" demonstrates how its author can happily lose himself in the contemplated object and thereby rediscover it for us in its mystery. Acrobatic exercises like "&," "O," "Games One *," and "Games Two:"— to be best understood as modern equivalents of the baroque emblematic composition practiced by the seventeenth-century English poet Francis Quarles — still confirm the resources of a cultivated imagination that can walk "on water" as well as on the tightrope.

Such exploits, thin as they are, point toward the accomplishment of "Juggler," with its pictorially dynamic sensibility. The related poem "Grace," which takes its cue from the religious poetry of G. M. Hopkins and therefore cleverly mimics his Saxon style at the outset, nimbly dances into Nijinsky's ballet acrobacy, thus making good the double meaning (sacred and artistic) of its title word: "flesh made word / Is grace's revenue." The holy man's "Grace" is superseded by the artist's "grace," hence the irony of a verbal inversion which secularizes the famous statement in the Gospel of Saint John ("and the Word was made flesh"). But in his dedication the secular artist tends, through hard-earned "grace," to re-attain lost "Grace"; and in the person of Hopkins, priest and poet, the two ideas expressed by one word became synonymous. "Lightness," describing a family garden scene, moves airily through cascading rhythms of accumulated clauses, and thus redeems its theme against the very complexity of meter and syntax. Lightness and grace are central factors of Wilbur's poetry as they were of Robert Herrick's, for whom the American has an avowed affinity. Sensuousness, wit, and prayer inform poems like "Bell Speech," and the intellectuality of "Mind," from *Things of This World*, avoids foundering in coldness by dint of a resilient purity which mirrors the excitement of imaginative adventure:

> The mind is like a bat. Precisely. Save
> That in the very happiest intellection
> A graceful error may correct the cave.

A "graceful error" which modifies our received notion of reality: that is an apt definition of Richard Wilbur's poetry, if not of all poetry.

A poet of Wilbur's generation who has shown much more stylistic restlessness is W. S. Merwin, for his four books of verse to date may be said to follow a recognizable evolutionary pattern. The first of these, *A Mask for Janus*, was published in 1952 in the Yale Series of Younger Poets under the editorship of W. H. Auden, the man who ever since coming to America has made himself felt as a unique shaping influence on the new American poetry. It is small wonder that Auden should have sponsored with a warm foreword the first book of a young writer who seemed intent on closed but flexible metric patterns, sophisticated vocabulary spiced with dry intellectual words, and mythical narrative.

Not that these traits guaranteed of themselves a breakthrough to genuine poetry; they were very much in the air, and could easily degenerate into fashionable affectation, of the sort today's unkempt rebels ascribe disdainfully to the surviving academic dandies. And Merwin's early endeavors, for all their technical versatility, do at times slip into a belabored language that sounds too self-conscious to be convincing, for it imitates the ease of lyric song and the profundity of *Gedankenlyrik* without attaining either. But the felicities

are frequent, even if sometimes they seem to stud rather than struc-
ture the poetic organism, and beyond the dated mannerisms one can
hardly miss the earnestness of basic tone.

Vision has often a hard time formulating itself, for it must struggle
with a great deal of literary artifice; when it does come through,
however, there is no denying its impact. And then the singing voice
provides the needed release. A loving study of folk poetry, recently
confirmed by Merwin's publication of *Spanish Ballads* as translated
by himself (1961), has helped him from the start in his effort to
achieve authentic lyricism of the kind that instead of parading in-
volved brilliancies takes the reader by surprise. His predilection for
fable as a form in itself, and not only as a seedbed of allegories, must
also be reckoned among the resources that this intellectually re-
fined poet musters to avert sterility. He has understood that if we let
the "naive" poet die out in us, we become literary Prufrocks, afraid
to bite into the peach of poetry, or into the apple of life. Therefore
Merwin's relentless fight with himself to overcome his own "literature" constitutes an exemplary episode in modern letters.

Realizing that this was the fundamental problem of his literary
generation, he has allegorized it as a collective experience, lived and
reported by a plural "We," in the long introductory poem of *A
Mask for Janus*: "Anabasis." An "anabasis," since Xenophon, has
been a long journey home through perilous uplands, from a dubious
battlefield, and toward the sea since the sea must be crossed to regain
home. Merwin's quatrains make it the inconclusive venture of the
modern mind into a no man's land where prolonged sojourn spells
death in life ("Anabasis (I)"), a shadowy condition to be possibly
overcome only at the price of seeing through the precariousness of
our most cherished myths ("Anabasis (II)"):

> We saw the islands of a new season.
> We were made young with watching, and our eyes
> Believed a garden and reserve where swung

> The fruits that from all hungers immunize.
>
> . . . .
>
> Our vision built on the approaching sand;
> We entered channels where the coral smiled,
>
> And but the countries of occasion found . . .

Mirages dissolve in the fever that aroused them, and we are left with "our fear," which becomes "A whirling without chronicle or end"; then in our alienation we are "the gesture of rages not our own," succumbing to tradition-bound or mass-bound ideologies, so that only "by violence" can we be "saved . . . from violence," and in the end we have "Our small language in the place of night," i.e. the something wholly ours we can oppose to obscurantism as our honest, if limited, contribution: the upshot of the circuitous adventure will be a thorough acceptance of our existential reality in the refusal to kneel down to mere fiction:

> Still we are strange to orisons and knees.
> Fixed to bone only, foreign as we came,
> We float leeward till the mind and body lose
> The uncertain continent of a name.

No haven is reached; we finally drift, in the recognition of our foreignness to the world, toward a release from all the tags of false individuation.

This final pose smacks of the decadent, but it does say that we have to live down our illusions, cultural or otherwise, if we want to attain some valid contact with reality. Disenchantment, this postwar god, marks Merwin's start on his career; correspondingly, his style will become less obviously literary and more and more dramatically direct, as a reading of his four books in chronological order shows. Like the modern poet he is, then, he starts his "anabasis" where others have ended — poets used to begin in naive enthusiasm and technical innocence, to progress toward technical refinement and philosophical disappointment or religious conversion, but in his case the reverse is true, for "We are children of a different curse." Yet, if like a Leopardi he has left all the myths behind, he will never do without myth, whether he submits it to the acid test of irony or develops it into a personal meaning.

Thus, in a long narrative piece from his second book, called "East of the Sun and West of the Moon" after a Russian fairy tale, the disappointing bird that initially croaks his ominous " 'All magic is but metaphor' " will be silenced in the end by the girlish voice of innocence regained which says antiphonally, " 'All metaphor . . . is magic,' " and this momentous inversion rehearses the trajectory of Merwin's poetry insofar as it is an expression of the quest for new wonder after wonder has been killed off in a rationally explained world. From experience to innocence: Blake's order is reversed, and the poet feels he has not lost his *raison d'être* in a society from which he had come to feel more and more estranged.

Hence the attitude of urbane irony, and the antithetic commitment to myth, are the two faces of the "Janus" that is the poet and, with him, modern man. They paradoxically coexist although (or because) one keeps arguing with the other. We find this precarious balance well articulated in "Dictum: For a Mask of Deluge," from the earlier book. The Flood will come, and it is a serious business; the ark is prepared, under darkening skies, while the dove rehearses its task — but the whole picture is presented hypothetically, with a gesture of skeptical detachment, as if it were all a stage action in a stage setting. Thus the apocalyptic message obliquely touching on our threatened age is delivered with reassuring wit — one thinks "it is not true, after all, it is only a fiction." But that is a mock reassurance. The man who "knows," who has seen through the emptiness of culture itself and says wearily, "All magic is but metaphor," is hungry for revelation, though he tries hard to deny or conceal the fact; and that revelation will come from poetry, for, precisely, "all metaphor . . . is magic." This is certainly the secret lore of the "Rime of the Palmers," to name another related poem from the same book, more lyrically than narratively oriented.

The Dancing Bears, published two years after Merwin's first book, shows him developing his central theme of fable versus disillusion ("What fable should I tell them, / That they should believe me?"; "I had come, / Unlooked for, from the shifting sea . . . / A field for doubting, my tales untrustworthy; / You believed, and therewith I was credible"). In pieces like "Tower" and "Proteus" he grafts some Yeatsian music on his own. Proteus, like the challenging Angel in the following poem ("Colloquy at Peniel"), is the elusive shape of our own mirrored self we keep trying to capture. The Cansos exhibit Merwin's more abundant rhetoric, frankly marred by an excess of abstract vocabulary; at the same time, his line distends freely to allow a suppler narrative form, unhampered by strict molds.

Accentual cadence keeps up the musical measure in a style which verges on the discursive. On the other hand, Merwin can still turn out carefully wrought lyrics in the patterns of closed prosody. His personal accent is strongly heard in a revelatory poem like "You, Genoese mariner," where Columbus becomes an alter ego of the poet with his creative "mistake." The image of the navigator as mythmaker appears also in the Jason of "When I came from Colchis," a fine accomplishment worthy of Pound, and Pound's sinewy phrasing comes to mind when one reads "December: of Aphrodite":

> (Vidal once, the extravagant of heart,
> For the love of a woman went mad, mad as a dog,
> And the wolves ate him . . .)

What has been said so far should not lead anybody to suspect Merwin of being a clever author of pastiches: a base of Auden and Valéry with a sprinkling of Hart Crane, plus much Yeats and some Pound. He accepts and uses these influences in the act of elaborating his own idiom; and that idiom rings increasingly surer in the remarkable achievement of *Green with Beasts* (1956). For here there is no question of eclecticism. Here language luxuriates in controlled abandon to sprout into heraldic animals like "Leviathan," whose hugeness is well expressed by the ponderous sentences and Saxon alliterations. Or like the "Blue Cockerel," a vision of pure wonder and delight:

> . . . Not Montezuma nor all
> The gold hills of the sun were ever so plumed
> As the blue of his neck, his breast's orange, his wings'
> Blazing, and the black-green sickles of his tail.
> It seems to be summer. But save for the blue hackles
> And the light haze of his back, there is no sky,
> Only the one tree spreading its green flame
> Like a new habit for heaven. . . .

Sumptuous color goes with sumptuous syntax, whose folds Merwin now drapes in masterly fashion. Contrived intricacies yield to a more straightforward utterance, which through syntactical reiteration can achieve the genuine epic note, as in "Two Horses":

> These have come up from Egypt, from the dawn countries,
> Syria, and the land between the rivers,
> Have ridden at the beaks of vessels, by Troy neighed,
> And along the valley of the Danube, and to Etruria;
> And all dust was of their making . . .

Biblical myths, like "The Prodigal Son" and "The Annunciation," are now treated without irony, as Rilke would; landscapes like "The Wilderness," "The Bathers," and others, have a firm edge.

The unwavering diction, opening up into unrhymed free verse, makes for the chastened seascapes (and inscapes) of *The Drunk in the Furnace* (1960), where Merwin beautifully exploits the possibilities of dramatic monologue. Melvillian tones are to be heard in the very titles —"Iceberg," "The Frozen Sea," "Sea Monster," "Deception Island"— and a ghostly whiteness lavished throughout again

recalls Melville's palette. Yet in the firmly outlined "family por-
traits" centering on Grandmother one feels above all the lesson of
Edwin Arlington Robinson. Merwin's "anabasis" has been a long
voyage home to directness and wiry simplicity, to the America of
his pioneer ancestors, as well as to their unfinished quest.

The fifties saw other serious poets emerge besides Merwin, and
anybody interested in the accomplishment or experiment of contemporary American verse should read at least Howard Nemerov,
David Wagoner, James Merrill (particularly for "The Bed"), Donald Hall (whose "My Son, My Executioner" has an enviably strong
neatness), Louis Simpson (endowed with a felicitous narrative
vein of epic possibilities), John Hollander, a literary sophisticate
among sophisticates (but see what earnest effects he can produce,
for instance, in "Late August on the Lido," with its final pun of ominous import that interprets Europe's decrepitude in the light of
Jaques's speech on the four ages of man, from Shakespeare's *As You
Like It*: "Europe, Europe is over, but they lie here still, / While the
wind, increasing, / Sands teeth, sands eyes, sands taste, sands everything"). Nor should one overlook Anthony Hecht, a devotee of
literary wit and strict metrical form who breaks through to a heart-
rending cry in the autobiographical poem "The Vow." This is a
feat of unobtrusive technical control where the closed stanzaic
molds seem to dam in the flood of grief over the poet's unborn child:

> Doctors of Science, what is man that he
> Should hope to come to a good end? *The best
> Is not to have been born.* And could it be
> That Jewish diligence and Irish jest
> The consent of flesh and a midwinter storm
>   Had reconciled,
> Was yet too bold a mixture to inform
>   A simple child?
>
> Even as gold is tried, Gentile and Jew . . .

In this passage, the italicized quotation from a number of ancient Greek poets in their disconsolate mood also serves to bring in the biblical austerity of Ecclesiastes, and thus joins stylistically "Gentile and Jew" through their respective cultural sources just as the Jewish father and the Christian mother were joined in begetting the hoped-for child. Urgent questioning and somber reply alternate, until in the conclusive stanza the voice of the stricken father will defeat despair by vowing to give life to another child. The best is still to reassert life, rather than "not to have been born."

In the recent effort of American poetry to dodge the shoals of bookishness, we can view the contribution of W. D. Snodgrass as an enduring one. Several of his poems were known long before the publication of *Heart's Needle*, the book that earned him a Pulitzer prize in 1960; he is careful rather than prolific, and unlike Allen Ginsberg, who pours out his talent in a wild endeavor to revive the Whitmanic posture as a defiance to the Establishment, Snodgrass chooses to refine, instead of discard, traditional technique. It is after all a matter of putting it in its place. Robert Lowell, whose courses in creative writing Snodgrass took at Iowa University, certainly did not teach him to despise craftsmanship, while Randall Jarrell, a later influence, advised him to loosen up his diction, to avoid showiness and concentrate on the personal.

Indeed, if we except some early poems on historical or mythical topics, like the Lowellian "Returned to Frisco, 1946," the finely written piece on Ulysses escaping the Cyclops' clutches by the trick of calling himself "Nobody," or the well-sustained "Orpheus," Snodgrass does write out of personal experience, and makes his poetry an outspoken plea for the personal in a world swayed by noisy slogans, encroaching industrial waste, and a heartless or shallow power-cult. He lets his "Cardinal" bird sing "for survival: / 'I want my meals and loving; / I fight nobody's battle; / don't pardon me for living.'" Here the protest is too pat to attain the level of poetry, but it characterizes Snodgrass' emphasis on the importance of indi-dividual life in his best achievement. Few poets are so unashamedly autobiographical, and this is in itself a gesture of courage in a cultural milieu overshadowed by Eliot's recommendation of impersonality. Yet the autobiography becomes, with Snodgrass, a way of focusing the public world and its basic issues; in "The Campus on the Hill," for instance, he projects his own experience as a teacher into the larger context of a world situation crawling with uncomfortable omens none of his comfortable students cares to recognize, and in "April Inventory" he satirizes the shams of academic bureaucracy, while the title series "Heart's Needle," composed of ten poems to his daughter by his first marriage, is played out against the insistent background of snow which implies, among others, the theme of cold war.

When one thinks of the barren game poetry threatened to become in an age of cultural saturation which felt uneasy about anything like lyrical candor, it is refreshing to hear a voice that says again "I" and means it, without masks or obliquities. The devil-may-care stance of Snodgrass in "These Trees Stand . . .," with the significant refrain "Snodgrass is walking through the universe," sounds like a new, and un-Whitmanic, "Song of Myself"— not the cosmic and all-inclusive self, that is, but the private, incorrigibly human self of the poet as Anyman. Humor of the ungenteel type, defiance, and emotional warmth go into the making of the second "Song," one of the most original love poems in our time:

> my love was near to spoiled
>   and curdled all my kindness.
> I find no kin, no child;
>   only the weasel's ilk.
> Sweet beast, cat of my own stripe,
>   come and take my milk.

Contemporary slang usage, according to which a "cat" is an unconventional person, may possibly lurk somewhere behind the feline imagery here.

This delightful impishness, which at times pours itself out into the looser measures of free verse, makes room for passionate lucidity in the ten poems of the "Heart's Needle" sequence, couched in regular stanza forms as if to stress the control of released emotion. Thus the firmness of rhythm and diction heightens the feeling. Instead of theorizing poetry as a "flight from emotion," like Eliot, Snodgrass sees and practices it as a *return* to emotion, the access being provided by ritual purification of the expressive medium. As a result, we have a directness of utterance which through its very simplicity avoids the pitfall of sentimentalism just as easily as it keeps clear of intellectualist artifice. Between this Scylla and Charybdis of poetry, Snodgrass navigates with assurance. The same assurance guides his interweaving of the private theme with the public concern. When his daughter Cynthia was born, the Korean war was still exacting its toll of human lives across the ocean. This historical predicament becomes, by a spontaneous symbolization, the objective counterpart of the poet's inner dilemma, torn as he was, during the winter of his daughter's birth, between commitment to his extant family and the imperious call of a new love that was to bring about divorce and a new marriage:

> Child of my winter, born
> When the new fallen soldiers froze
> In Asia's steep ravines and fouled the snows,
> When I was torn
>
> By love I could not still,
> By fear that silenced my cramped mind
> To that cold war where, lost, I could not find
> My peace in my will . . .

The birth of a new human being is contrasted with the simultaneous death of many others, and at the same time subtly linked to it by the focal use of "new fallen," where "new" ironically suggests the child, and "fallen" sharply offsets the implicit analogy, while also evoking, perhaps, an idea of ripe fruit — the maturing decision in history and in the writer's mind. But the birth of the baby also parallels the birth of new love, and the death of soldiers fighting in Korea underscores the death of the old love. Winter provides an appropriate seasonal setting for the crisis, since it seals a cycle and makes a new one possible. Winter and snow — a recurrent background theme in the poems — naturally connect the psychological and domestic conflict with the world situation which impinges on so many private lives, and so the political commonplace "cold war" resonates with a new meaning in the intimate sphere of the writer's own heart. By wrenching a headline cliché from its staleness into personal relevance, Snodgrass has made it the imaginative hinge between individual and historical reality in the poem. For "cold war" is the *cramping* political deadlock all over the world, as well as the different kind of war waged on the snowy mountains of Korea, both meanings coming to their focus in the unresolved torment of a lovesick man. "War" and "peace" designate here states of mind, but their historical import is only too vividly present, thereby reminding us that the politics of love can be as cruel as public politics is.

The way Snodgrass develops these seminal cues in the rest of poem No. 1 of the series makes for thematic enrichment without confusion or dispersal. For he expands the snow symbol to include the innocent blankness of the baby's mind, unaware of impending trouble, and then objectifies that mental metaphor into the snow-covered landscape which the farmer ranges with a contented eye, believing in its apparent immunity from any dangerous violation. The protective quilt on the child's bed and the awaiting white page of the writer are correlated to that Homeric digression in such a way as to reinforce the central idea of suspense. Cold war is a prolonged, intolerable suspense, and suspense is what the poet knew

26

that winter while the inward struggle had not yet manifested itself or reached the eventual decision.

The actual Korean war recurs in poem No. 3 to counterpoint the autobiographical situation. Just as in Korea, at the armistice table, they "sever and divide / Their won and lost land," the divorce settlement in America formalizes the estranged couple's separation; "Prisoners are returned" over there, while here the one child belonging to both parties cannot be permanently returned to either, short of a Solomonic judgment. Thus, of course, "nobody seems very pleased," even if "what must not be seized / clenches the empty fist." The tenseness lingering on in such a precarious resolution had been announced in the first stanza by the uncommented street scene of a child who, upon coming to a puddle, hangs on his parents' hands: "They start / At the live weight and lurch together, / Recoil to swing him through the weather, / Stiffen and pull apart." Though the political picture is there for the sake of an expanded comment on individual existence, the final allusion to Solomon reflects in its turn on the condition of the world at large: Korea's partition was itself a Solomonic judgment, along with the other cold-war divisions one readily associates with it. "Divorce" then prevails in modern politics and is synonymous with cold war for mankind. By concentrating on his own personal problems, Snodgrass has been able to understand something important about the problems of the world he has been cast to live in — poetical analogy being the instrument of understanding.

But the contrapuntal analogy does not mechanize itself into a repetitious device. Poem No. 2 directs our attention entirely to the now three-year-old child intent on rudimentary gardening, and to the anguish of the father anticipating its imminent departure. A variation on the same theme appears in poem No. 4, while poems No. 5 and No. 6 also concern themselves exclusively with the poignant intimacy of father and daughter. To be sure, analogy (of a nonpolitical kind) clinches poem No. 5 to make the fox in a wintry landscape a counterpart of the father who has had to pay for his domestic freedom with his dearest good — the child, who is a part of himself as the trapped paw is a physical part of the untamable fox:

> Where he backtracks and sees the paw,
> Gnawed off, he cannot feel;
> Conceded to the jaw
> Of toothed, blue steel.

This memorable ending develops from a lullaby song line quoted in stanza three: "*Fox / Went out on a chilly night* . . ."

Animal imagery, so congenial to the child's magic world, constellates all the poems of the sequence and dominates poem No. 9 in particular, occasioned by a casual visit to the museum of natural history some time after the little girl's last departure. Animal magic here acquires a sinister overtone because the creatures are dead, a motionless semblance of life:

> walking to kill my time once more
> among the enduring and resigned
> stuffed animals . . .

Aesop's, Phaedrus', and La Fontaine's fables mirrored the vagaries of human behavior in live denizens of forest or field, but Snodgrass, reviewing the museum halls, reads his personal and historical moral in a weirdly lifelike lifelessness. The stuffed beasts symbolize his past: the snarling bobcats have to do with his divorce, the bison shoving at his calf reminds him of the obedience he imposed on the little girl, the "lean lioness" watching her cub with unrelenting alertness is a tacit emblem of the divorced mother, the great elk locked in mortal combat suggest, beyond the idea of marital wrangling, the paralysis imposed on West and East alike by cold war — and the white bears in the "ocean of broken ice" confirm the suggestion before the poet explicitly elaborates on it.

A bitter irony brings home the dreadful implications when the poet, wryly perverting the sacramental formula of marriage, says of the fighting elk that "Whom equal weakness binds together / none shall separate," and of the bears that they are "Yet separate . . ." The apocalyptic review arouses shudders of horror when it comes to human and animal embryos "curled / in jars of alcohol." The visitor has been trying to "kill time," and time is *killed*, to be sure, in that several possibilities of life have been stifled by inevitable cruelty. The "unborn" are, in a sense, his might-have-been children, and in another, the unrealized future of our world. The last poem concludes the sequence on a note of relief: living animals responding to the invitation of the season, and the ever-present daughter, whose interval of absence had made the museum scene so poignantly horrid. Snodgrass has certainly learned from Robert Lowell as profitably as Lowell himself from Allen Tate — thus demonstrating the vitality of what is by now an American tradition in modern poetry. It is by no means casual that the "Heart's Needle" sequence begins with winter and ends with spring.

James Wright, who published his first book of verse in 1956 and the second in 1960, cannot be ignored by the discriminating reader, if only because his commitment to ethical truth has made his style develop toward a kind of passionate directness that parallels Snodgrass' typical achievement. The very frequency with which he posits his own undisguised "I" in the poems bears witness to a sense of literary and human responsibility. Since Wright fully acknowledges the common bond of humanity in sin, he can become, not Christ, but "Saint Judas," in the title poem of his second book:

> Then I remembered bread my flesh had eaten,
> The kiss that ate my flesh. Flayed without hope,
> I held the man for nothing in my arms.

And in "At the Executed Murderer's Grave," from the same volume, he converses with the dead criminal, unsentimentally, for that man, as a figure of deviated destiny, is after all an anti-self, and the paradoxical identity a Whitman would have affirmed in naive effusiveness takes on a much more harrowing shape, as it were beyond guilt or forgiveness:

> Wrinkles of winter ditch the rotted face
> Of Doty, killer, imbecile, and thief:
> Dirt of my flesh, defeated, underground.

These are memorable accents, and Wright is often memorable in his conversations with the dead, really a form of self-questioning which makes him an existential poet. This aspect seems to mark the important direction of his striving for a personal statement, though the poems inspired by the wonder of nature or by the charm of American folklore are by no means negligible; those like "Evening" and "At the Slackening of the Tide" breathe the astonishment of unguaranteed existence – human life is there, but gratuitously, so to speak, on the brink of nothingness. Mannerisms lingering on here and there in part of his work are clearly not going to be in the way, and his current experiments with open form in free verse authorize bold expectations about this poet's future achievement, since he refuses to "stay put."

The same is true of Galway Kinnell, whose first book (*What a Kingdom It Was*, 1960) evinces, however, more richness in imagery and attitudes along with greater unevenness in accomplishment. An exuberant nature, Kinnell can be termed what Wright could not – an American Expressionist; and with this goes a readiness to risk the prosy and the informal which places him closer to the Beats than any of the poets discussed so far. He writes in looser cadences than Wright or Snodgrass: free verse, often conversational, and seldom rhymed. Following the advice of Dr. Williams and Robert Bly, he seems to prefer accentual rhythm to the time-hallowed iambics they resent so much. The syntax, as important a factor in his poetry as it is in Merwin's, is relaxed, save in a few poems where it swells into complex units for special effect; the clauses generally align themselves in the simple patterns of coordination, subordinate constructions being relatively infrequent. This makes for ease rather than tautness in his diction and rhythmical movement. One could say he tends to build his poems by accumulation and expansion, not by compression as so many of his contemporaries do; an extreme example of this is the long descriptive piece on New York which concludes the book, "The Avenue Bearing the Initial of Christ into the New World." A Whitmanic spirit moves this expressionist endeavor to seize the throbbing and shrill variety of New York life, and the incidental failures of thickness, loose diction, and commentary are Whitmanic too. Failures or no failures, however, the poem represents a gesture of courage; one can see in it the pledge of greater future accomplishments on the part of a young poet who dares to write richly instead of curling up in early preciosity. Kinnell brings a gust of fresh air into American poetry, without indulging in vulgarity.

Nor does he have to affect the pose of ignorance in order to capture the freshness and the freedom found in American outdoors life; see for instance the flavor of landscape in "First Song," "First Communion," "Westport," "Alewives Pool," and "Leaping Falls," while the savage episodes of "Burning" and "The Wolves" remind us of Mark Twain roughing it, and maybe of the readable part of Jack London — notes toward an American epic. Rhythmical energy conveyed by elastic stress, pictorial vividness, and syntactical resilience make "Leaping Falls" a poem hard to forget. The "downrush" of the cascade comes through by virtue of the headlong movement of syntax, which encompasses in one sentence the twelve lines of the first two stanzas. The next two stanzas offset this dynamic picture by presenting the falls frozen, "draped / Without motion or sound, / Icicles fastened in stories . . ."

The description is enhanced by the break-up of discourse into

31

brittle short clauses, like icicles: "Cold was through and through, / Noiseless. Nothing / Except clouds at my nostrils / Moved. Then I uttered a word, / Simply a bleak word / Slid from the lips. . . ." As if cracked by that word, "A topmost icicle came loose / And fell, and struck another / With a bell-like sound, and / Another, and the falls / Leapt at their ledges . . ." In this fifth stanza the movement of syntax becomes continuous again, to render the temporary animation of falling icicles. The one sentence that sweeps through this stanza spills over into the next and last, where the "outbreak of bells" raised by the crackling ice finally "rings and ceases." The spell of winter has been only apparently broken, and

> The silence turned around
> And became silence again.
> Under the falls on the snow
> A twigfire of icicles burned pale blue.

Poems like this are possible only when one responds with joyous attention to nature. The ritual mystery of a bird killed and eaten on earth, then subjectively mirrored in a constellation, suffuses "To Christ Our Lord," which concludes with a breathtaking effect:

> He wondered again, for whom had love stirred?
> The stars glittered on the snow and nothing answered.
> Then the Swan spread her wings, cross of the cold north,
> The pattern and mirror of the acts of earth.

"At the Reading of the Poet's Will" combines an impish wit with prayerful earnestness, the alloy being made possible by choppy lines and vivacious rhymes:

> I took Christ for my pattern,
> Once he was kind to a slattern,
> If I was led into mazes
> Blame and praise Jesus. *Amen.*

To sample further, "A Toast to Tu Fu" redeems its bluntness through hearty Rabelaisian humor:

> And again to you, Tu Fu,
> For gorging at the feast
> Honoring your rescue,
> For not mentioning virtue
> In your short speech, nor praising rot,
> And for having had the appetite and timing
> To die of overeating on the spot.

Not many writers are capable of such a liberating gesture today; and the poem will reveal a remarkable subtlety behind its blunt façade when one considers the effect of imitative suspense the second stanza achieves by widely separating the words "and for" from their dependent locution "having hung on like a bear" in a context which portrays the hero's dogged clinging to life against odds.

Flaming imagery reminiscent of Van Gogh's paintings makes "Lilacs" a truly expressionist poem, to reassure those who fear too much sophistication may have dried up the language of American poetry:

> The wind climbed with a laggard pace
> Up the green hill, and meeting the sun there
> Disappeared like a piece of warm wax
> Into the ground. Down on the south slope
> A bitch stretched, and swaths of fierce lilacs
> Opened astonishing furnaces of scent.

Pictorial and tactile sensuousness helps to create animistic personifications of natural forces like wind and sun, to the point where they become demonic. "Furnaces of scent" is a resultant image one cannot help gleaning.

Instead of this torrid delight, pretty evenly spread, we find a gradual heightening of motif and tone, from initial toughness to final prayer, in the complexly articulated eleven quatrains of "Easter." While taking its cue from local chronicle — the murder by drowning of an anonymous nurse — this fine poem rehearses a favorite theme of some European poetry, namely Rimbaud's "Ophélie,"

33

Benn's "Schöne Jugend," Heym's "Ophelia," and Brecht's "Of the drowned girl." The meter itself, consisting of free accentual verse in alternately rhymed quatrains, recalls Brecht's composition. But the difference of treatment far outweighs these similarities, which may or may not be intentional.

The beginning establishes a factual tone that couldn't be drier, through the reportorial language of the newspaper: "We read of her death in the morning. / By the riverbank shreds of clothes and her purse. / Raped, robbed, weighted, drowned — / They conjecture the night-off of a virgin nurse." The "we" taking in the sinister news is rather uninvolved; these are curious citizens who idly comment on the published crime over their breakfast. "We read . . . they conjecture": curiosity and detachment are equally stressed. When the collective speakers of the poem cross the un-Jordan-like river and reach the church to hear their minister's Easter sermon (stanzas two through five), the mood of detachment persists, aggravated by the boringly predictable words of the clergyman:

> . . . he is talking of nothing but Easter,
> Dying so on the wood, He rose.

Of course the joke is also on the bored worshipers, for "nothing but Easter" does not necessarily have a belittling implication, and if belittling, then it belittles their shallow minds too.

In stanza four the description of the partly restive, partly absentminded congregation cunningly exploits for the sake of humor the sacramental cues furnished by the sermon's inevitable theme: they think of the ghastly "morning news" (and not of the Easter message, which also is "morning news"), they regret that they "rose at all" (from bed and not, like the resurrected Christ, from the grave), they, again in a very un-Christian way, are "dying on the hard wood of the pews"— a wood which is no cross. The ceremony becomes a parody of ritual; the minister's voice is "disinfected," and "Death is everywhere" (stanza 5), instead of the much-talked-about

34

esurrection. Both the horrible crime reported and the perfunctory celebration of an archetypal ritual, along with the river polluted by village swill and, farther downstream, by industrial waste, bring out the appalling desecration of modern reality, against the holy theme. There can be no real Easter in our world.

Stanza six, geometrically central to the poem, brings us back to the river, where on (ironical) "Walden calm" the boats "are fishing" with wire hooks for the submerged corpse. They are fulfilling, in a sadly literal way, Christ's exhortation to his fishermen Apostles; they are fishing for a corpse, not souls. We realize that this quatrain is the structural hinge of the composition when we notice that after it the mood changes from negative to positive; the speakers are now fully awake to the grievous reality, having left behind their morning routine, and they no longer refer matter-of-factly to the drowned girl in the third person, but address her first in the tone of earnestly unliteral question ("Up through the mud can you see us / Waiting here for you, for hours, / Virgin lady, trapped or working loose . . .?"), and finally in the passionate tone of exhortation, climaxed by pure prayer:

> Do not, moved by goodbyes, be altogether sorry
>
> That the dream has ended. Turn
> On the dream you lived through the unwavering gaze.
> It is as you thought. The living burn.
> In the floating days may you discover grace.

Thus, in the reversal of attitude, the sacramental mood appropriate to Easter is introduced, but on the human level, outside the church, and in the drab contemporary setting the speakers take now the posture of a religious choir. Among the felicities of this second part one cannot pass up the pivotal use of the verb "rise" (stanza eight) to mean the hoped-for surfacing of the still unretrieved body. Such use lifts from their officially religious context the words of the Easter sermon quoted above, but only to soak them in actuality and thereby revitalize them. This is a positive irony, hinting at the Christlike aspect of the victim, and not a negative one as in the deflating humor of stanza four ("Some of us lament we rose at all")

Since the partial affinity with Brecht's poem on a similar theme was mentioned, it seems fitting to observe now that while the German's work moves from an objective tenderness to a final estrangement or *Verfremdung*, his young American rival's lyric goes the other way round, from marked estrangement to involvement, as if to imply that even in a desecrated world the sacramental values can be restored under the form of human commitment. Georg Heym's poem comes to mind, because of certain details and the over-all sweep one feels in reading Kinnell's conclusion, which again achieves his grand "largo" effect by encompassing more than three stanzas in one sentence, fluvially sustained through the reviewed "stations" of the floating body's downstream voyage – until the short clauses at the very end seal that movement in majestic peace.

If two German Expressionists have seemed relevant to a discussion of what is perhaps Kinnell's best poem to date, that confirms my earlier suggestion about a general definition of his style. With regard to theme, the contrast between desecrated reality and apocalyptic revelation is treated very strongly in another fine poem "The Supper after the Last," where Christ surrealistically appears to shatter man's fleshbound crassness, although (or because) He is "becoming a mirage." Comparison with Merwin's analogous themes will show how much more temperamental Kinnell's Dionysian imagination is, and how the dangers it must beware of are of a very different nature from those Merwin's Apollonian intellectualism has been facing.

Chronology would advise against coming to John Logan after his younger contemporary, especially if we remember that Logan's first book, *A Cycle for Mother Cabrini*, dates from 1955, but ideally

peaking the transition is not inappropriate, for Logan's concern
with personal reality and with the possibility of the holy in an un-
holy world, so close to Kinnell's own interests, has led him to develop an even freer and equally muscular style in his more recent
book (*Ghosts of the Heart*, 1960). Logan is Irish by extraction and
Catholic, and the combination is notoriously explosive. His verse,
more strictly devotional in the first book, less exclusively so in the
second, has the violence we could expect in these circumstances,
with the attendant unevenness that disturbs an unrelenting ear.

If at times the verse shows a coarser grain and sags under the bur-
den of prosiness, the surprises it often holds in store for readers with
an unsqueamish taste are enough of a reward. Like Brother Antoni-
us, the religious poet from California who concentrates on Dionysian intensity of utterance, Logan is sometimes associated with the
Beat movement, and in fact he has published in the *Evergreen Review*, a journal so very partial to the Beats, but in many ways he
could also be compared with Thomas Merton and Robert Lowell —
the Lowell of the most recent phase. Violent imagery, to celebrate
the violent gentleness of feminine sainthood, flashes forth from the
Mother Cabrini hagiography:

> And the air in the high Andes
> Was thin and lucid as milk
> Or fire, or as violets she sailed
> In boats in Lombardy,
>
> A child afraid of the water
> But sick for the fire and milk
> Of the sea's wake and for the souls
> That flashed like fish . . .

As in Kinnell, the lines are accentual, sustained by their strong
stress — really music in the ears of Dr. Williams! In other parts of
the sequence, off-rhyme is cleverly used, with a muted effect that
saves the rhymed quatrains from mechanical lilt:

37

> And chose a cheap ring,
> A piece of junk but something
>
> Your sisters sell; to me
> Its feel and pull heavy
> On my fingerbone wore
> In for a time, the terror
> Of your delicate flesh, the scant
> Weight within the fragrant
> Bones . . .

Sharply run-on lines, creating at times, in the bridged interruption from line to line and stanza to stanza, a syncopating effect comparable to the use of sudden pauses and percussion in modern music vivid paradoxes, high pitch, and, at the same time, common speech – these are basic traits of Logan's poetry, and if one looks for strength he has it, even if sometimes at the price of form. But then, "form" in poetry should not be equated with "good manners."

There is literary merit in the readiness of men like Logan to bite into the raw flesh of experience, as there is vitality in the way he posits his own self in a dramatic confrontation with existence and with the holy ("I thank God Mother Cabrini's / Body is subject to laws / Of decay. To me it is / A disservice when flesh / Will not fall from bones / As God for His glory / Sometimes allows. I speak thus / For flesh is failing: / That it shall fall is my / Salvation . . .") This insistence of the naked "I" in the poetry of Logan, of Wright Kinnell, and Snodgrass, marks a turn away from the earlier dominant cult of the "mask," of Yeatsian restraint and Eliotic indirection, and it goes with the swing of the poetical pendulum in America from elegance to violence, from understatement to loud outspokenness. Of course we can find in Eliot, and even more in Pound, the headwaters of both currents, but for some time their lesson had been interpreted as one of distant formality. Charles Olson's poetics of "projective verse," the latest important manifesto, names Pound (and Williams) as a model.

If in his earlier book Logan sang hymns to the Italian nun who had displayed a tireless energy in populating the whole American continent with hospitals and other charity institutions badly needed by so many immigrants (and that certainly makes her a culture heroine worthy of high praise), *Ghosts of the Heart* sees him broaden his scope. Whereas the figure of the hermit or of the saint as hero of the Impossible dominated the 1955 effort, now he celebrates as a secular saint the poet at loggerheads with the world: Heine, Rimbaud, Hart Crane (to be sure, Saint Augustine and the English martyr Southwell had also been men of letters). And besides, he explores his relation to his own family and to the world, in poems which assume a more relaxed pace, at times also prosier.

Certainly the biography of Rimbaud, whom Logan sees as a "negative" saint in his unsparing lunge toward the absolute, is vigorously sung, with an unfailing rhythmical impulse:

> He tried in the bird the rule
> Of the snow, the peculiar look
> Of flutes: so much the worse
> For the boy who flies his home
> And god and verse, for the brass
> That wakes a horn. The weight
> Of the gold about his waist
> Shall make him sick. The horizon's
> Shift of blue is a change
> In the man. And the verse will clutch
> And cast. And the apter alchemies
> Of God make one change last.

That is the wiry last stanza of an eleven-stanza poem which does credit to its author's ability to keep up his epic breath, while his treatment of the poet as hero avoids easy pathos as well as tiresome sophistication. Poems about poetry, or about the poet himself, have become commonplace in our age, but here Logan breaks through the cocoon of literary narcissism to give us the existential predica-

ment of the poet as man; and his complementary piece "Narcissus:
Vision and Retrospect" shows the poet with his "skull in [his]
hands," as if the lovely self-involved youth of Greek myth had
turned Trappist.

The companion piece to "The Lives of the Poet" is about Heine,
and again shows mettle. It is hard to ignore the sheer energy of diction in passages like this:

> He tried to kiss his father's
> Hand but his pink
> Finger was stiff as sticks
> And suddenly all of him shifts —
> A glorious tree of frost!
> Unburdened of the sullied flesh.

The nervous alliterations, the vowel echoes that suggest rhyme
without formalizing themselves as such, the mobility of accent —
and the sudden, liberating metaphor of the tree, which fuses the
archetype of the Tree of Life, the visual idea of the skeleton, and
the tactile sensation of cold in feverish shudders, as in certain poems
by Emily Dickinson: these traits are impressive. The tree image is
resumed in the following stanza to announce oncoming death:

> In the last years of his life
> He wept at the pain of lust
> Stirred in his tree-like limbs
> Already dry. And he left
> Framing with paralyzed lips
> One more note to his mother.
> Only the ambiguous Dumas cried
> At the holy rite they danced when he died.

Alternately tight and loose, the utterance strikes us as dynamically
alive, and the cultural references (there are many in this poem) are
effortlessly woven into the fabric of song.

Romantic urge is checked by caustic diction, and the result is a
very credible tone of clear-sighted involvement. The conclusion, in

stanza ten, transmogrifies a Lorelei statue, related to Heine's poem on the Rhine enchantress, into an ambivalent siren-mother figure which also has to do with art itself and Melancholy (this last mythical personification probably coming straight from Albrecht Dürer's famous etching):

> Powerful over the figure
> Of the frantic Harry, and over the
> Three mother-fishes:
> Melancholy, an idol of the Hebrew Smart,
>
> And one with the mended, broken arm of Art.

Since Heine's obsessive relation to his mother counts for much in this poem, it will not be difficult to see how autobiographical it is when one reads the next piece, "On the Death of the Poet's Mother Thirty-Three Years Later," which transposes that relation to the personal sphere of Logan's own experience of sonhood. Here his Roman Catholicism, his devotion to the mother he never knew, and his rebellious approach to art come to the forefront in the language of confession; he says he "nursed / At a violent teat with the boys / Of the bronzed picture." In the poet's private memory, the bronze emblem of the she-wolf suckling the twin founders of Rome shades into the Irish setter which amused and protected his first childhood, "Arched over [him] a God-like Bitch."

If Heine's life as told by Logan was a flight from mother, Logan's instead is a perpetual quest for his lost parent, and the quest quickens his allegiance to a geographically remote Church, to the absent Divine Mother from across the sea: Mother Cabrini, Thetis, "mother-fish" Lorelei. The versification, we notice repeatedly, tends to the crepitant Saxon patterns: "Yet I was not so *scared* / Or *scarred* I *co*uld not / *Scream* and *cli*mb to find / My aunt to *cry* for help . . ." In this, Logan is not far from another Catholic poet, G. M. Hopkins, though unlike Hopkins he has had the chronological opportunity to absorb Freud in his system. The dubious chance denied his great predecessor could have ruined him as a poet, but it didn't. Freud is assimilated and criticized, inasmuch as poetry can be a critique of any kind. Poetry is above all, for Logan, confession and epic, and so we can say that his free rendering of *Iliad*, Book I, in "Achilles and the King," is also autobiography — though not of the diffuse kind, as some of his later pieces unfortunately tend to be. Achilles the man of anger, and Achilles the lonely son seeking consolation from his secretive mother, the sea-goddess Thetis, are the two faces of John Logan himself, who in this "translation" is writing again "the lives of the poet." A poet has nine lives, like a cat — perhaps even more.

So has American poetry, whose persistent vitality in these post-war years the present survey has, it is hoped, significantly sampled. The available harvest is so rich that one cannot avoid grievous omissions. And that is not the only handicap incurred by an endeavor of this kind, for many writers, whether discussed here or not, are likely to add so decisively to their contribution as to make a change of appraisal necessary. Granting that any conclusions in such an unstable situation can only be tentative, one could say that the analyses here of some representative young American poets show a tendency to move from the heaven of "pure" poetry to the purgatory of existential poetry; and this affords comparison with what has been developing in postwar Italy and France.

Olympic Wilbur formally opens the era of the postwar generation by recommending confinement of the Dionysian genie in the bottle; Merwin strives to find a way out of the impasse of intellectualism by an existential self-criticism of intellect; Wright and Snodgrass do not just look at the world or think about it, they suffer and act in it, and thus reformulate the theme of man as naked existence, though without quite breaking the "bottle" of traditional discipline;

and with Logan and Kinnell the genie starts to emerge from the bottle, perilously trying for new expansions and new shapes.

Though some of the most promising new poets, like X. J. Kennedy (*Nude Descending a Staircase*, 1961), refuse to release their pressing genie from the "bottle" of rhymed iambics, others do let the genie out, and, in the case of many Beats, it is in fact rampant. *The Opening of the Field*, Robert Duncan's latest book, shows what the genie can do if granted his freedom; Duncan's visionary power is as undeniable as Blake's was, and his plea for open as against closed form, on the strength of Pound's and Williams' example, is far from empty. More concentrated than Duncan, less daring perhaps, but also less prone to slips into rhetoric, Denise Levertov has been emerging as an American poet of the first order since her transplantation from England. Fear and wonder, joy and awe crystallize with her into acts of poetical vision that embody a new fidelity to experience, a clarity of focused perception to be envied by writers of the tumultuously visionary kind. And I would also mention Gary Snyder and Jack Hirschman as poets whose work gives evidence of the promise that lies in this forceful gesture by which American poetry is seeking to recapture the restless experimental spirit that made its modern "renaissance" so exciting, from 1912 through the mercurial twenties. The mid-century composure was not its last word.

⌐ Selected Bibliography

Anthologies of Verse

Fifteen Modern American Poets, edited by George P. Elliott. New York: Rinehart, 1956. (With a short foreword by the editor and biographical, bibliographical, and textual notes.)

Mid-Century American Poets, edited by John Ciardi. New York: Twayne, 1950. (With a foreword by the editor.)

Modern American and Modern British Poetry (revised, shorter edition), edited by Louis Untermeyer in consultation with Karl Shapiro and Richard Wilbur. New York: Harcourt, Brace, 1955.

Modern Verse in English, 1900–1950, edited by Lord David Cecil and Allen Tate. New York: Macmillan, 1959. (A comprehensive survey of British and American poetry, with critical introductions and biographical notes. Allen Tate's introductory essay is fundamental, and particularly useful is the presentation of some postwar American poets like Wilbur, Nemerov, Nims, and Whittemore in the larger context of poetry in the first half of the twentieth century.)

The New American Poetry, 1945–1960, edited by Donald M. Allen. New York: Grove, 1960. (With a short foreword by the editor, bibliographical notes, and an appendix of "Statements on Poetics," among which Charles Olson's on projective verse, Robert Duncan's, and Robert Creeley's stand out.)

The New Poets of England and America, edited and selected by Donald Hall, Robert Pack, and Louis Simpson. New York: Meridian, 1957. (With an introduction by Robert Frost.)

Poesia Americana del Dopoguerra [Postwar American Poetry], edited by Alfredo Rizzardi. Milan: Schwarz, 1958. (A bilingual anthology with the English texts and Italian translations, biographical and bibliographical notes, and a very detailed introductory essay by the editor, later included in his critical study *La Condizione Americana*.)

Poets of Today, edited by John Hall Wheelock. New York: Scribner's, 1954 to date. (An annual anthology of three new poets, with an introduction by the editor. Volume I (1954) includes Harry Duncan, Murray Noss, and May Swenson; Volume II (1955), Norma Farber, Robert Pack, and Louis

Simpson; Volume III (1956), Lee Anderson, Spencer Brown, and Joseph Langland; Volume IV (1957), George Garrett, Theodore Holmes, and Robert Wallace; Volume V (1958), O. B. Hardison, Jr., Kenneth Bitchford, and Sheila Pritchard; Volume VI (1959), Gene Baro, Donald Finkel, and Walter Stone; Volume VII (1960), James Dickey, Paris Leary, and Jon Swan; Volume VIII (1961), Albert Herzing, John M. Ridland, and David R. Slavitt.)

Individual Books of Verse

Ciardi, John. *As If: Poems New and Selected.* New Brunswick, N.J.: Rutgers University Press, 1955.

Creeley, Robert. *A Form of Women.* New York: Jargon Books, 1959.

Duncan, Robert. *Selected Poems* (1942–1950). San Francisco: City Lights Books, 1959.

———. *The Opening of the Field.* New York: Grove, 1960.

Everson, William ("Brother Antoninus"). *The Residual Years.* New York: New Directions, 1945, 1960.

———. *The Crooked Lines of God: Poems 1949–1954.* Detroit: University of Detroit Press, 1959.

Ferlinghetti, Lawrence. *Pictures of the Gone World.* San Francisco: City Lights Books, 1955.

———. *A Coney Island of the Mind.* New York: New Directions, 1958.

Ginsberg, Allen. *Howl, and Other Poems.* San Francisco: City Lights Books, 1956.

Hall, Donald. *Exiles and Marriages.* New York: Viking, 1955.

———. *The Dark Houses.* New York: Viking, 1958.

Hecht, Anthony. *A Summoning of Stones.* New York: Macmillan, 1954.

———. *The Seven Deadly Sins.* Northampton, Mass.: Gehenna Press, 1958.

Hirschman, Jack. *A Correspondence of Americans.* Bloomington: Indiana University Press, 1960.

Hollander, John. *A Crackling of Thorns.* New Haven: Yale University Press, 1958.

Jarrell, Randall. *Selected Poems.* New York: Knopf, 1955.

Kennedy, X. J. *Nude Descending a Staircase.* Garden City, N.Y.: Doubleday, 1961.

Kinnell, Galway. *What a Kingdom It Was.* Boston: Houghton Mifflin, 1960.

Kunitz, Stanley. *Selected Poems 1928–1958.* Boston: Little, Brown, 1958.

Levertov, Denise. *Here and Now.* San Francisco: City Lights Books, 1957.

———. *With Eyes at the Back of Our Heads.* New York: New Directions, 1959.

Logan, John. *A Cycle for Mother Cabrini*. New York: Grove, 1955.
———. *Ghosts of the Heart*. Chicago: University of Chicago Press, 1960.
Lowell, Robert. *Lord Weary's Castle*. New York: Harcourt, Brace, 1946.
———. *The Mills of the Kavanaughs*. New York: Harcourt, Brace, 1951.
———. *Life Studies*. New York: Farrar, Straus and Cudahy, 1959; New York: Modern Library (Random House).
Merrill, James. *Country of a Thousand Years of Peace, and Other Poems*. New York: Knopf, 1959.
Merton, Thomas. *Selected Poems*. New York: New Directions, 1959. (With an introduction by Mark Van Doren.)
Merwin, W. S. *A Mask for Janus*. New Haven: Yale University Press, 1952.
———. *The Dancing Bears*. New Haven: Yale University Press, 1954.
———. *Green with Beasts*. Chester Springs, Pa.: Dufour Editions, 1956.
———. *The Drunk in the Furnace*. New York: Macmillan, 1960.
Nemerov, Howard. *Mirrors and Windows*. Chicago: University of Chicago Press, 1958.
———. *New and Selected Poems*. Chicago: University of Chicago Press, 1960.
Nims, John Frederick. *Knowledge of the Evening*. New Brunswick, N.J.: Rutgers University Press, 1960.
Rexroth, Kenneth. *The Signature of All Things*. New York: New Directions, 1949.
Roethke, Theodore. *Words for the Wind, the Collected Verse*. Garden City, N.Y.: Doubleday, 1958.
Shapiro, Karl. *Poems, 1940–53*. New York: Random House, 1953.
———. *Poems of a Jew*. New York: Random House, 1958.
Simpson, Louis. *A Dream of Governors*. Middletown, Conn.: Wesleyan University Press, 1959.
———. See *Poets of Today*, Volume II.
Snodgrass, W. D. *Heart's Needle*. New York: Knopf, 1960.
Snyder, Gary. *Myths & Texts*. New York: Totem, 1960.
Swenson, May. *Cage of Spines*. New York: Rinehart, 1958.
———. See *Poets of Today*, Volume II.
Wagoner, David. *Dry Sun, Dry Wind*. Bloomington: Indiana University Press, 1953.
———. *A Place to Stand*. Bloomington: Indiana University Press, 1958.
Wilbur, Richard. *The Beautiful Changes*. New York: Harcourt, Brace, 1947.
———. *Ceremony and Other Poems*. New York: Harcourt, Brace, 1950.
———. *Things of This World*. New York: Harcourt, Brace, 1956.
———. *Advice to a Prophet and Other Poems*. New York: Harcourt, Brace, and World, 1961.

Wright, James. *The Green Wall*. New Haven: Yale University Press, 1956.
──. *Saint Judas*. Middletown, Conn.: Wesleyan University Press, 1960.

Critical Studies

American Scholar, vol. 28 (summer 1959). Issue on Contemporary American Poetry.
Gorlier, Claudio. "La nuova poesia americana: maturità e accademia," *Ulisse* (Florence), vol. 38 (September 1960). Issue on Western Poetry Today.
Greene, George. "Four Campus Poets" (Wilbur, Viereck, Jarrell, Lowell), *Thought*, 35:223–46 (1960).
Hoffman, Daniel J. "Arrivals and Rebirths," *Sewanee Review*, 68:118–37 (1960).
Jarrell, Randall. *Poetry and the Age*. New York: Knopf, 1953.
Jerome, Hudson. "Poets of the Sixties," *Antioch Review*, 19:421–32 (1959).
Parkinson, Thomas, ed. *A Casebook on the Beat*. New York: Crowell, 1961.
Rizzardi, Alfredo. *La Condizione Americana* [The American Condition]. Bologna: Cappelli, 1959.
Rosenberg, Harold. *The Tradition of the New*. New York: Grove, 1961.
Rosenthal, Macha Louis. *The Modern Poets*. New York: Oxford University Press, 1960.
Times Literary Supplement (London), November 6, 1959. Issue on The American Imagination.

Journals

CRITICISM of contemporary American poetry and/or the poetry itself may be found in numerous periodicals, among which the following are especially useful: *Poetry* (published monthly in Chicago since 1912); *Beloit Poetry Journal* (published quarterly in Beloit, Wis.); *The Sixties*, formerly *The Fifties* (published irregularly in Madison, Minn.); *Contact* (published quarterly in Sausalito, Calif.); *Big Table* (published irregularly in Chicago); *Chicago Review* (published quarterly in Chicago); *Black Mountain Review* (published from 1954 to 1957 at Black Mountain, N.C.); *New World Writing* (published until 1959 in New York); *Evergreen Review* (published bimonthly in New York); *Botteghe Oscure* (published in Rome from 1949 to 1960); *Accent* (published quarterly in Urbana, Ill.); *Prairie Schooner* (published quarterly in Lincoln, Neb.); *Chelsea* (published quarterly in New York); *Paris Review* (published in Paris); *Quarterly Review of Literature* (published quarterly at Annandale-on-Hudson, N.Y.); *College English* (published monthly in Champaign, Ill.); *Kenyon Review* (published quarterly in Gambier, Ohio); *Partisan Review* (published bimonthly in New York); *Hudson Review* (published quarterly in New York); *Sewanee Review* (published quarterly in Sewanee, Tenn.); *Saturday Review* (published weekly in New York); *New York Times Book Review* (published weekly in New York). A valuable reference is *Index to Little Magazines* (Denver, Colo.: Alan Swallow, 1948–59), the first five volumes edited by Harriet Colegrove, the later ones by Eugene P. Sheehy and Kenneth A. Lohf.